MOSS SIDE, MANCHESTER 1950S/1960S

Nostalgic Memories

ALAN WILLIAMS

ISBN: Softcover 978-1-5434-9200-2
 Hardcover 978-1-5434-9201-9
 EBook 978-1-5434-9202-6

Print information available on the last page

Rev. date: 03/14/2019

To order additional copies of this book, contact:
Xlibris
0800-056-3182
www.xlibrispublishing.co.uk
Orders@ Xlibrispublishing.co.uk

INTRODUCTION NO 1

It may seem a little strange to have 2 introductions for the same book but after mum wrote her first book on "Victoria Baths," she began writing her second book on Moss Side, Manchester.

I always promised her, I would complete this book in her memory and have made an attempt to carry this out.

Mum & I in Antwerp, Belgium (May 10th 1947)

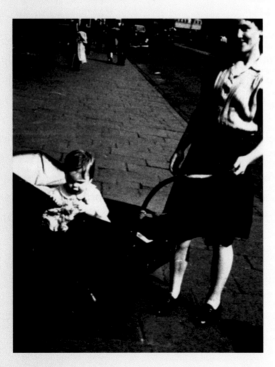

Mums first book had been produced and inspired by a television series called "Restoration" which showed an impressive swimming baths in Manchester, being saved by a number of volunteers who wanted to save the building, as it fell into a terrible state of neglect and was heading for being bulldozed as many of the buildings around had endured.

The television program in 2003 won the competition and gave the baths a fantastic amount of money to carry on the work.

For many years, I had encouraged mum to write a book on Moss Side in Manchester, but she had always avoided doing this due to other pressures in life.

I always knew that she was capable of writing a book as she had written lots of short papers whilst she was training to become a teacher at the age of 38.

After writing her first book called "Victoria Bath's Manchester's Water Palace" she began writing her second book on Moss Side, Manchester, but never managed to complete it due to ill health and eventually died on New Year's Eve 2009.

Mums introduction and the first three chapters of this book are as she wrote it, but before I start writing chapter 4, I have included a letter mum wrote to her Auntie Ethel in 1940 about leaving Belgium for England. The 4[th] chapter onwards are my memories of growing up in Moss Side as a child, not realizing how difficult it must have been for my parents to rise up against the many challenges ahead.

The different style of thought and writings are quite significant but I hope it achieves what I have set out to do and show how an area of Manchester has changed, from the people who lived and grew up there, to the way our memories remember Moss Side in the 1950's, onwards. I am now in my 70's and can only put into this book, my memories as I recall them. I hope people will find it entertaining and possibly bring back memories for people who went through similar experiences to me, with the shortage of money and the hope of a better life after the 2[nd] world war.

Mum was born in Ipswich in 1920 and always had a burning ambition to become a teacher. Her mum and dad had moved to Belgium when her mum became ill with diphtheria. They thought the air would help with her recovery, but it didn't really help and she eventually died. Her dad later remarried a Belgium lady and mum and her sister Lucy, continued to live; go to school and generally had quite a privileged life, as her dad became Managing Director

of the large Schwepps factory in Genval, near Antwerp. After school days, both mum and Sister Lucy worked in the syrup laboratories in the factory.

But that was about to change when the family were forced to leave Belgium and head for Britain at the start of World War 2, when the Germans invaded Holland and Belgium. I have included a letter which mum wrote to her Aunty Ethel in 1940 which tells of the journey back to Britain.

Mum had all the qualifications she needed to go to Teacher Training College but she was to find out later, that she would need to re-sit all her exams again as they were not recognized it Britain. This meant she would have to put her ambitions on hold. It would take a long time before she could get back to the point of going to Teacher Training College.

Mum was only a young lady when she had left Belgium in 1940 and on arriving back in England, she joined the Wrens.

She met my dad, who was a serving sailor in the war and came from Tonyrefail, Portypridd in Wales. They were married in Exeter, Devon in Feb 1944 and had 2 children. Trevor was born in Dec 1944 and I was born in Antwerp in May 1946. At the end of the war, Mum had gone back to Belgium, living in Antwerp as my dad was still trying to get his de-mob papers. When he finally was de-mobbed, he was unable to find any work in Belgium and so they made the decision to come back to Britain in the hope of finding work and bringing the children up in a fairly stable environment.

A view of the Schwepps Factory in Genval, Belgium in 1983

A view of The Schwepps Factory in Genval, Belgium in 1995

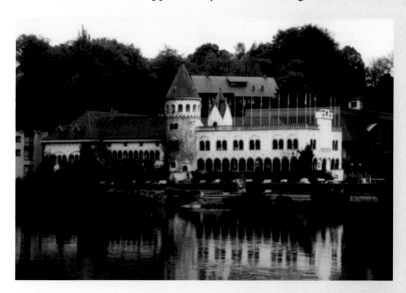

The Factory Genval, Belgium, Sept 2012
(Now a hotel)

1 of Mums upstairs room in the Schwepps Factory in Genval, Belgium - Sept 2012

Just to explain a little about the factory, mum mentions in the letter of 1940. The factory in Genval, Belgium, was owned by Schwepps and mums father was the managing director at the factory.

He had his own rooms upstairs in the factory where my mother and her sister Lucy, also lived.

Mum and Lucy had steady jobs working in the Syrup Laboritory at the works downstairs.

The works looked like a castle, in fact, it was known as a castle, with a huge lake at the front.

Many years later in 2012, I went to see the castle & stayed for a few nights as it had now been turned into a hotel. You couldn't help but admire the tasteful way this building had been looked after and by special permission, I was allowed to go upstairs a take photographs of the rooms which had been occupied by our family, before the war had started.

These were mums notes that she wrote down as a diary whilst getting back to England in 1940. From these notes she wrote her letter to her Auntie Ethel in Poole.

Fri 10[th] May 1940 Invasion of Holland & Belgium. Air battles & bombing overhead. Went
to work

Sat 11[th] May Went to work till lunchtime.

Sun 12[th] May. Much as usual. Still heavy bombing. Some British soldiers billeted with us.
Mon 13[th] May. BBC News sounded encouraging. Refugees from places near German front
were coming through village. No communication with Antwerp either by telephone or post.
No traffic permitted on roads.

Tues 14[th] May. French soldiers arrived, very surprised to find us English citizens still there. Genval had been evacuated, even local authorities. Our letter from Consul must still have been left lying in Genval County Hall. Just as we were going to have dinner a lot of Brit. soldiers came in and took possession of factory. The officers took our flat and we had ¼ hour to put a few things on the one remaining lorry, food, clothes, money, I took some books. Dad filled lorry tank & 4 tins with petrol and we set out for Antwerp. Went to Antwerp Schwepps Office where Dad picked up our wages and the letter from Consul. Went to Consulate but they had gone as had all the other Britons and no more ship coming to port. Stepmother's parents had left for France 2 days previous. Decided to try Ostend in morning.

Wed. 15th set off to Ostend. When we got to Ghent we were stopped by Brit troops who told us the Germans had taken Ostend. We had to follow the road to France. Met the Newtons at small village in W. Flanders. BBC news good so decided to stay next day.

Thurs. 16th. Still German planes overhead being harassed by ours.

Fri 17th & Sat 18th had to stay by order of military as no civilian traffic allowed on roads - Heard rumble of German guns. BBC reported Germans has broken through.

Sun. 19th. We set off for France at 6 in morning hoping to get a ship to England. Mr. Newton also came away with us. Spent all day trying to get across French border. Somewhere near Ypres we found a room at last.

Dad advised by War Graves Ass. & YMCA to get to the French frontier by 6 next morning.

Mon 20th May 1940. As we passed through a village on way to frontier a baker's shop was just opening so I dashed and got 4 loaves.
When we got to the road where we would be allowed to cross we found a long file of cars which had been waiting all night. Let in 50 at a time. We were on that road from 7 to 1 o'clock until at last we got across. Passed through Dunkirk Centre Square crowded with refugees. Run out of petrol Mr. Newton towed us. That night horrific bombardment of Dunkirk. We stopped at a farm. Already some 80 people sleeping in the barns so we just made ourselves comfortable on the lorry. To our great surprise the farmer came out and invited us to have his spare room! Dad managed to get a few litres of petrol while we were at the farm

Tues 21st May. - Set off after breakfast to Calais. Had what we called dinner, biscuits, bread & butter. Dad went off to search for petrol. As he came back, he met a Scotsman who told him a destroyer had docked and would be leaving for England in ¼ hour. Bundled our few bits into sheet bundles and set off for quay, despite horrific bombardment and machine gunning. Had to dive under trucks several time. Once on board in the calm of H.M.S. Venomous it only took us an hour to get to Folkestone to a lovely welcome and the best cup of tea I've ever tasted. Then on to London. Slept at "Empress Hall" while all us refugees were checked next day. We decided to go to Newport Mon. to friends as we thought for sure England would be invaded and Ipswich was too near the coast.

Sunrising Bungalow,

Melstock Road,

Oakdale,

Poole,

Dorset

28.11.40.

Dear Auntie Ethel,

As you see by the address we are now in England. It was of course only after a lot of adventures that we did arrive here. When the Germans marched into Belgium on Friday 10ᵗʰ May we decided to stay in Genval and keep the factory going for the time being, until we should know for sure which way things would go. So Friday and Saturday we went to work and didn't take much notice of the numerous air battles going on overhead. The Sunday passed in much the same way as usual, except that we did not go far from the house so that we could make a dash for shelter if it should be necessary, and another feature of these days was that we usually had the dinner or tea ready (hot on the table) and we would have to go down to the cellar because of some nearby bombing, and of course when we came back up again, everything would be cold. The English soldiers had been arriving since the Saturday and on Sunday we had some billeted with us. Monday passed in the same way and as the news reaching us seemed encouraging we decided to stay on. On this Monday though, lots of refugees from the places near the German frontier were already passing through our Village. All this time we couldn't get any communication with Antwerp either by telephone or post, and we learned afterwards that there was no traffic permitted on the roads. On Tuesday some French soldiers arrived at our place; they were very surprised to find us there still, as our village had been evacuated - everyone had gone even the local authorities and our letter from the British Consul summoning us back to England must still be lying about somewhere in Genval, because we never receive such a letter. Well just as we were going to have dinner, a lot of English soldiers came in and took possession of the factory and the officers took our flat as their quarters, so now we had to get out. We had just about a quarter of an hour to pack up a few things and get going. We had one lorry left in the factory so with the help of the soldiers, we loaded our things on it and filled 4 tins of petrol and set out for Antwerp.

We took some people with us, in fact every available inch on our lorry was used for passengers all the time we were on the way. We meant to go to Antwerp and then get a boat from there to England and take Mummy's parents with us. Well this part of the journey was quite easy going, as there were not many refugees on the road yet. We reached Antwerp by evening and first went to the factory where we found a letter for us from the Consul. I suppose the Consul must have sent us another one as we had not got in touch with them yet. Daddy went to his office but

discovered everyone had gone with all the other British subjects from Antwerp and there were no more British ships coming to Antwerp.

Then we went to Mummy's parents' house but the people there told us that they had left two days before for France. They had not been able to get in touch with us either and I suppose they had thought that we had already left. So as we could not get over to England from Antwerp we decided to try Ostend the next day. Although I slept soundly that night it appears that it had been a pretty noisy one, not only bombing but also street fighting between German parachutists and the Belgian police. These parachutists were dressed in all kinds of uniform, and that night most of them had Dutch uniforms on.

The next morning we set out for Ostend. The going was not so easy now as the stream of refugees was visibly swelling. All went well until we got to Ghent and then we were not allowed to continue on the road to Ostend. It was no use arguing with the police and saying that we had to return to England, we had to follow the refugees on the road to France. Ghent was badly damaged already, in fact we had already passed through the town before I realized it was in fact Ghent. I had not recognized it and we went on driving all through that day and towards evening. As we were driving through a small village in west Flanders, we saw to our surprise a friend of Daddy's, a Mr. Newton, also an Englishman who worked at Schweppes, so of course we stopped and as it was getting late, we decided to stay there for the night. After a long search we were lucky to get a room at a farmhouse; they were very nice and kind people. We went to listen to the BBC news on a neighbor's wireless and as they said the Germans were being held back we decided to stay there the next day. Mr. Newton had been there in the village the last two days. He, his wife and her parents had also left Antwerp in their small car and were on the way to France, but as the news seemed heartening they were staying in this village for the present. The next day passed without event, except for the usual planes overhead of course. The Germans had already developed a healthy respect for our planes. The next two days we had to stay where we were whether we wanted to or not, as the authorities had issued orders that no civilian traffic of any kind was allowed on the roads of Belgium; this was to enable the military to move without being observed by the refugees.

By the evening of our third day in this village, we got news by the BBC that the Germans had broken through all the defenses and were advancing rapidly in a southward direction from Holland and from the east from Germany. Both Antwerp and Brussels had by this time been taken, so we decided to get going the next morning as early as possible. Later in the evening our anxiety was further increased by a low menacing rumble in the distance which crept slowly nearer and nearer; this was the noise of the artillery and tanks of the advancing Huns. It was on this last day in this village that I saw some of the Belgian soldiers returning from the front; they were in tiny groups of 5 or 6, usually from totally different regiments. They were what was left of the regiments that had to withstand the

first of the German onslaught. They told of how they had been attacked on three sides, from the front by the tanks, which nothing seemed to be able to stop. These tanks just came on and on and the Belgian soldiers had seen their wounded comrades being crushed to death. Then they were being continually bombed and machine-gunned from the air, and as if that was not enough, they were being shot at from behind from the houses. The so-called Belgian civilians living in them had hoarded up guns, machine guns and ammunition to use against their own countrymen. It is incredible to what extent pro-Nazi agents carried on activities over there. These soldiers that we saw had had no food, hadn't slept or had a shave since the beginning of the war. They had no orders as to where to go; the army was completely disorganized and the soldiers just wandered aimlessly about and these soldiers were no exception. It was the same wherever we went; so the collapse of France and Belgium did not come as a very great surprise to us. Well the next morning we set out at 6 o'clock according to plan. Mr. Newton also left with us and we decided to make for France and try to get over to England through the first French port that we got to. The going was very slow now as the road was jammed with all kinds of vehicles, there were ice-cream carts, bicycles, all sorts of cars and lorries, farm carts, prams, wheel-barrows and even scooters, all piled high with household goods. Our car could only advance a few hundred yards, then we would have to stop and wait a few minutes. There was a line of refugees on foot walking beside us and the same people kept overtaking us, in fact they got along much faster than we did. Of course we now presented a lovely target for the German planes, and indeed they made the most of their chance and swooped down now and again to release a few bombs.

Food was another big problem as what we had brought with us was by now running out. We still had part of a tin of biscuits left and some butter. Bread was almost unobtainable and you could always tell where a baker's shop was by the crowd that collected outside waiting for the loaves to come up. Meat was not available, but eggs seemed to be on sale everywhere, indeed we ate so many of them on the road, that we do not mind the shortage of them now. Most people pulled up turnips and rhubarb from the fields and ate them as they went along.

By noon we had got to within 2 or 3 miles of the French frontier, but the French had a marvellous way of shutting the frontier to refugees just as we were approaching it; then they would advise us to try another place, some 5 or 6 miles distant and of course by the time we reached there, that place would shut. We spent the whole day in this way, first trying one place then another. This would not have been so bad only it was draining our petrol supply and of course all the petrol pumps had been emptied long ago.

Night came on and we were still on Belgian soil, so we decided to start the almost hopeless task of searching for lodgings. We went from house to house, but everywhere we got the same answer 'they were already full up'. At last one place where we asked, they advised us to try the house opposite as there was room there, but when we knocked

the people were out, so we waited until they came home and asked them for rooms. Luckily they had two, so Mr. Newton had one and we had the other. (They were also very nice people.)

We were now somewhere near Ypres and as there were a lot of English clubs and associations there. Daddy tried getting in touch with them and at last, through the YMCA we were advised to get to the French frontier by 6 o'clock the next morning as we would be allowed through then. So the next morning we set off at about 4 o'clock through places well known through the last war - Passchendaele, Mount Kemmel, Ypres, etc. There was as yet no traffic on the road and we travelled along at a nice speed. We had a car on tow now, someone who had run short of petrol.

As we were passing through a village they were just opening a baker's shop so I made a dash for 4 loaves of bread.

Well, we reached the road where we were allowed to cross the frontier and found there one long file of cars that had been waiting there all night. They were letting these cars pass in groups of about 50 at a time as they had to examine passports and things like that. We waited on that road from 7 until 1 o'clock until at last it was our turn.

We were not so very far from the sea now so we thought we might be able to reach Calais the same day. Our petrol ran out though, so we had to leave the people we were towing and Mr. Newton had to tow us. We passed through Dunkirk now and the big square in the centre of the town was crowded with refugees all sleeping on the pavement.

That night in a terrific bombardment of this town, the Germans dropped tons of bombs amongst these people; that is the way Germany was protecting Belgium against the savage English.

That night we stopped near a farm and as there must have been already about 80 people sleeping in the barns, we did not even attempt to get lodgings. We made ourselves comfortable on the lorry and were just going off to sleep when the farmer came out and to our great surprise, invited us into his house. Of all the people sleeping around his farm, he chose us to offer his spare room, so we certainly did consider ourselves lucky. Perhaps it had something to do with the horseshoe I had found and put on the lorry - I'm always sorry that I forgot to bring it over, as it would have been a nice souvenir. Well we gratefully accepted his offer of hospitality and even though I slept as usual on the floor rolled in a blanket, I slept as soundly as usual. They told me next morning that the whole farmhouse had been rocking on its foundations by the terrific explosions coming from Dunkirk, but I heard nothing of it. Daddy had been able to get a few litres of petrol the evening before, so the next morning after breakfast we set off for Calais. Looking back we saw a low dense black cloud of smoke overhanging Dunkirk, an ominous reminder of the havoc wrought the night before by the Nazis.

We reached Calais by noon and made straight for the Consulate. A lady there told us that the consul was trying to get a ship and that we were to return there at two. To fill in the time we had what we called our dinner, which meant biscuits, bread and butter and then in case we could not get a ship, we went in search of petrol. Daddy was just coming back to the lorry with his petrol when he met a Scotsman who asked him if he was not leaving with the destroyer. Of course Daddy asked what destroyer and he told him that one had just docked and would be leaving at 1 o'clock - it was then a quarter to 1. This meant there was no time to lose, so although there was an air-raid on, we drove down to the quayside with machine gun bullets whistling round our ears. Added to this was the fact that Lucy and me (we were sitting on the back of the lorry) were almost thrown off because of the craters in the road. When we were nearly at the quay we had to stop and get under the lorry as the Germans were now diving down upon us. Well the AA guns drove them off and we started getting our things off the lorry. We happened to have two new bed sheets with us, so we tore one of them in two and bundled everything into them. Then while we were waiting for the gangway to be lowered, someone told us that we had to go to the other end of the platform to get a ticket. Mr. and Mrs. Newton, Daddy, Lucy and me went down there and just then some bombers came along. The shelters were around the other side of the building and it seemed ages before we could reach them. The few remaining panes of glass were all breaking, but we managed to reach shelter before the really near bombs came. Lucy had a tin hat on, she had been lent by a French sailor, and it came in handy when bits of the ceiling started falling. The noise was terrific and the lights had gone out. I heard after a terrific bang, the sound of crumbling masonry very near and some people screaming. I really thought that it was our place that had been hit, but then things quietened down and I realized that we had somehow escaped again. My first thoughts were of Mummy and Rachel whom we had left on the quayside and I made anxiously for them. To my great relief I saw them crawling out unhurt, from under some railway trucks.

There was another big crater at the farther end of the platform and a block of buildings that had been there when I went to the shelter, had vanished completely.

Before we could get on board though, we had to dive under the trucks twice more. Out there in the open the explosions were even more deafening and although I put my hands over my ears, I was almost deaf for about a ¼ of an hour. The blast of one explosion blew off a sailor's hat and I remembered picking it up and handing it back to him.

Eventually we did get on the ship and as the bombers were still overhead and were just releasing a couple more bombs, a sailor pushed me down a stairway-to what we thought was comparative safety - but I had to laugh when I found that I had landed just were all the ammunition was stored.

From now on everything went smoothly. Within ¾ of an hour we were at Folkestone. There we got a lovely welcome and were given bread and cheese, cakes and what seemed to me to be the best cup of tea I had ever tasted.

From there we went to London and then we went to Newport as we thought that Ipswich would be evacuated.

Daddy and me got work eventually at a mineral works. Daddy as a salesman and I in the syrup room. Now Daddy has been transferred to Poole as Foreman and so we have moved down south - it's a lovely warm climate down here.

I hope you are getting on alright in Ipswich. Do please write and tell me how things are there. So hoping to hear from you soon.

I remain with lots of love

Yours Prudy xx

Mrs. Pru Williams (MUM 1920-2009 Prudence Williams)

INTRODUCTION NO 2

In the beginning there was a Marsh or Moss, a swampy tract of land, outside Manchester, of little value to any, save the few farming families who battled to eke out a meagre living from this inhospitable land.

Things had changed a lot by the time I first arrived in Moss-Side, Manchester, soon after the Second World War.

I had been in the Wrens, but soon after I married Bill in 1944, I found I was pregnant and, as the Navy puts it, I was "Discharged to Shore." No such thing as Maternity Leave, and resuming one's career after the baby was born. We just accepted this as the norm. Until I could either afford child-care, or, as it turned out, the children, were old enough to go to school, I was destined to stay at home and be a full-time Mum.

I didn't mind, I had always had ambitions to become a teacher and had started my studies, but the war interrupted and, as I said, I joined up. I must use this time wisely I thought, until such time when I would be able to resume my Teacher Training course at University.

Bill was still in the Navy and my first priority was to find a home for him to come to when he was de-mobbed. I had tried various bed-sit arrangements with family and friends, but nothing suited us really until I wrote to my sister's mother-in-law, Rose Wilson, who lived in Manchester.

I knew as soon as I read her welcoming letter that the two boys and I would be very happy living in Moss-Side, Manchester.

Rose met us at Exchange Railway Station, then a busy, thriving complex, now long demolished. Again, I felt the warmth of her welcome and knew that Manchester was to be my new home.

Rose took us by bus to Greenheys Lane, pointing out the various landmarks on the way. I could hear the pride in her voice as she made sure we saw and admired the very high Dunlop's chimney of their factory in what I now know is Cambridge Street.

As a former mill-worker she was proud of her city and the way it had developed and prospered on the wings of cotton. She had prospered too, by her hard work and thrifty savings she had set herself up in business as a successful publican and had helped her sons to do the same.

Rose had organized everything for us. She insisted that we must move into her house in Ridley Grove. She had arranged to go to stay at her son's at Victoria Hotel until such time as it took me to find a suitable flat or house we could afford to rent. She had even enlisted the help of one of her neighbors to prepare a very welcome meal for us after our long journey from my friend's house in Belgium.

We enjoyed the meal and even more the relaxation and the happiness of realizing that here, in Moss-Side, Manchester, we were being cared for and our worries were not only smoothed over but swept away as being of no account. All Rose was concerned about was that we should accept her very generous hospitality and make ourselves at home here.

I loved Manchester from the moment I saw its lovely soot-blackened, but beautifully-built Victorian works, warehouses and shops. It did not take me long to find an apartment in Fernleaf St., which we could afford. As our belongings had now arrived, courtesy of the Manchester Ship Canal, we were able to move in there.

We had no money of course, but Bill had been promised a job at the Red Tower Brewery, so we had prospects. He turned down the brewery job, in favour of working as a heavy-goods driver for British Rail.

The first few weeks were hilarious. Our table was a big packing case, our chairs, the smaller ones, but we invited Rose and her friend to a meal, which I enjoyed cooking and we all had a lovely time, laughing at the past and making plans for our future.

I was so happy here, exploring the local area and its lovely parks, the little Rec., Alexandra Park, and, going a bit further, Platt Fields and Whitworth Park. We walked for miles and I really got to know our wonderful surroundings and the many good friends I had made since coming here.

This is the reason why I want to write this book. So many nice people live here, that it always seemed such a shame that the place is only known to the outside world by the headline-grabbing news items, caused by a small minority, but which give the area such a bad reputation.

For me, Moss-Side will always hold a warm place in my heart. Coming here was like coming home, even though I had never been here before.

Now that I have moved away, due to family commitments, I always feel the need to return, which I do on a regular basis. I have helped at St. James' Church Hall on Princess Road with my Local History Exhibitions and I have kept in touch with my friends. When I have visitors, from other parts of Britain or from overseas, I like to take them to see where I lived when I first came to Moss-Side.

There is so much potential here, the University complex is near, the theatres, the music scene, the libraries, the museum, all within walking distance. With so much culture and history around, it is small wonder that people are inspired to use their creative talents. They sing, they dance, they write, they act, they become inventors, sportspeople and musicians. Moss-Side has produced and is still producing a plethora of famous people.

Chapter 1

Development of Moss-Side.

Moss-Side or, "The Moss-Side," as it distinguished itself among the hundreds of Mosses which covered a large part of Lancashire, was a late developer as a township. Not that this worked to its disadvantage, quite the opposite.

At the time of Sturges Bourne's Act of 1819 which stated that the clergy, churchwardens, overseers, and not more than twenty, nor fewer than five substantial householders or occupiers, elected annually by the ratepayers, were to constitute a Select Vestry.

In Moss Side, however, there were no churches, no clergy, no churchwardens, nor so far as can be traced, any overseers. As to substantial "householders," there were 172 in 1821, and 208 inhabitants in 1831, living in 34 houses. It is therefore very probable they did not bother themselves about Bourne's Act.[1]

Moss-Side developed slowly during the first half of the 19th century.

'The first Moss Side Ley Book, (rates book), begins March 28th, 1835, after the passing of the Poor Law Act, 1834. The Overseers used to meet at the Waggon and Horses Inn at Longsight, that being the only public building in the township.

The earliest highway payment was made, July 28th 1836, "Paid George Lings for the township of Moss Side Highway Ley, 16s. 2d."

In the same year as Bourne's Act (1819), another Act expressly declared that there were then no highways in Moss Side and no Highway surveyors had ever been appointed for that township.[2]

So, at the time of Bourne's Act, Moss Side was still a very rural area.

1 Chapter 1 'Old Moss-Side' by H.T. Crofton
2 "Old Moss Side" Chapter 1 p122 by H.T. Crofton

Mrs Gaskell's description of Mary Barton's Farm, although written in 1848, brings the Arcadian aspect of early 19[th] century Moss Side vividly to one's mind.

She writes, "There are some fields near Manchester well known to the inhabitants as Green Heys Fields," through which runs a public footpath to a little village about two miles distant. In spite of these fields being flat and low, there is a charm about them. Here and there an old black and white farmhouse. Here may be seen haymaking and ploughing. You cannot wonder, then, that these fields are popular places of resort at every holiday time, and you would not wonder if you could see or I properly describe the charm of one particular style, that it should be on such occasions a crowded halting place.

Close by it is a deep clear pond, reflecting in its dark green depths the shadowy trees that bend over it to exclude the sun. The only place where its banks are shelving is on the side next to a rambling farmyard belonging to one of these old-world gabled black and white houses I named above, overlooking the field through which the footpath leads. The porch of this farmhouse is covered by a rose tree, and the little garden surrounding it is a medley of old-fashioned herbs and flowers. This farmhouse and garden are within a hundred yards of the stile, leading from the large pasture field into a smaller one, divided by a hedge of hawthorn and blackberry, and near this stile on the further side there runs a tale that primroses may be found and occasionally the blue sweet violet on the grassy hedge bank.[3]

By the time Mrs Gaskell wrote this vivid description of Moss-Side of the early 19[th] century, many changes had taken place there.

"Greenheys - a mile from the centre of Manchester was pure country. De Quincey, (1785-1859) recalled the district as it was when his parents possessed one of the few houses there, says that he was brought up "in the sweetest of solitudes" and refers to it again as a "rustic solitude"[4]

There were many reasons for all these changes from "rustic solitudes" to a thriving, busy little township, adjacent to Manchester as we will see in the next chapter.

3 Extract from Mary Barton" Chapter 1 first 2 pages)
4 A Biography of Manchester by Rachel Ryan, p67

Chapter 2

Further Development of Moss-Side whether as the saying goes, "It's something in the air," or, in the water maybe, in swampy Moss-Side, but the people there, although coming from many different backgrounds, have two things in common. A pride in their area and strength of character to meet and overcome all difficulties.

As we have seen, there had been many difficulties for the residents of Moss-Side to overcome in the early 19[th] century.

At that time it was a very sparsely populated area. The people who lived and worked there, mainly farmers, had to contend with the poor quality of the marshy soil, and the fact that there were no proper roads, just a few lanes, which must have become very muddy and difficult to negotiate, especially in winter.

The 1820 map of the Parish of Moss Side, by Johnson, confirms this. Although the area named as Moss Side seems more extensive than it is today, the farms and houses were built mainly on the borders, leaving the centre to marsh and field.

Where Moss Side Lane meanders southward through Hulme, to enter Moss Side, in the fields and small hamlet of Greenhill, now only recalled by a street named after it, off Greenheys Lane. There, Johnson's map shows a small cluster of three buildings. Several more are marked along Clock House Lane, (as Johnson names Moss Side Lane) in the Greenheys area.

[5]Henry Crofton writes, "It is perhaps needless to say that Moss Side Lane is now called Moss Lane East but it has in the course of time been called a great many names, some of them far from complementary before it was put in its present condition. It has been variously known as Moss Lane, Moss Grove and Clock House Lane".

Pepper Hill Farm is also noted on the 1820 map. The farm has long gone, but it lives on in the memories handed down through the generations by people who knew the farm or the pictures and paintings of it, one of which used to grace the wall of Moss Side Free Library. "This is the black and white-drawing of Pepperhill by Tavaré which was presented to the library by Mr John Livery of Whalley Range. Another local picture was preserved there, namely an

5 'Old Moss Side,' by H.T. Crofton p. 7

unpublished drawing of a scene in Greenheys, by Ralston, dated 1827. The scene includes a view of Coffin Bridge, which was situate at the end of Warwick Street, near Denmark Road."[6]

The development of Moss Side is closely linked with that of Manchester's booming cotton industry.

"Almost from the beginning of Manchester's great prosperity, more than a hundred years before, her richest citizens had tended to build their houses on the fringes of the town; constantly removing, for the sake of health. Greenheys, a mile from the centre of Manchester, was pure country. Thirty years later, the egress of wealthy men was in full swing.[7]

It soon became apparent that this 'removing' was favoured to be in a southward direction, towards the Cheshire countryside.

Johnson's 1820's map shows that Hulme was rapidly being covered by rather haphazard street patterns, and, as we know from the condition of the housing which survived, it was of poor quality. But more housing was needed and the large tracts of fields and countryside by the side of the Moss began to be viewed by planners and builders. It would be difficult land on which to build.

In a description of the Pepper Hill Farm area, written in 1911, the author quotes, "it was a land of pools, many of them scattered about the fields, a score or more, fatal in their treacherous depths to many[8] young bathers."

A fuller description of these "Twenty Pits" is given in another old book, with the explanation as to how they originated. The author quotes "almost all the maps cited indicate by the numerous 'pits' dotted over the District, the old practice of marling the mossland, when it was being brought into cultivation. Moss Side could boast of its "Twenty Pits" the marl out of which enriched the owner of the Lloyd Estates."[9]

The farmers would want a good price for their fields. Many pools and ponds would have to be drained, but it was in the right southward direction.

So progress was slow, but very necessary.

6 'Old Moss Side" by H.T. Crofton. p. 20
7 "A Biography of Manchester" by Rachel Ryan p67
8 'Concerning the 'Mary Barton' fields by John Morthner.' p7.
9 "Old Moss Side" by H.T. Crafton p.3

By the 1840's, people in authority on local and national level were concerned about conditions in the new industrial towns.

In 1841, Dr. Richard Howard, Physician in Ancoats and Ardwick Dispensary, gave a stern warning:

"Until the labouring classes are supplied with the commonest necessaries of life, relieved from their state of extreme wretchedness and destitution which habitually exist, fever and disease will continue to prevail extensively among them.[10]

By this time, Edwin Chadwick had published his scathing report on the sanitary conditions in large towns, which led to a demand for government action, and in 1848, after a further enquiry of its own, Parliament passed the first Public Health Act which led to the establishment of Local Boards of Health.

Moss-Side, by now an established township, was fortunate to have caring, responsible members on their Local Board, who not only ensured that the paving, sewers and clean water supply to the houses were provided, but also that the bye-laws on building procedures were strictly adhered to.

This resulted in a much better quality of housing in Moss Side, much of which has survived to the present day.

The Board was also very much aware of the importance of education and set up its own School Board. Its elections were vigorously contested, the various religious denominations joining in the campaigns.

By the time the first National Survey map of Moss Side was published, in 1851 we can recognize an orderly development of streets. These streets were lined with terraces of well-planned, well-built houses of the standard required by the Moss Side Board. They had large, airy rooms with good light and ventilation, bathrooms and indoor flush toilets, some had small front gardens.

It was along the main roads, Greenheys Lane, Princess Road, Alexandra Road, Upper Lloyd Street, Moss Lane East, Moss Lane West and Great Western Street that further important and rapid changes took place in the second half of the 19th century.

With an ever increasing population moving into Moss-Side, it was along these main roads that the public services were to be found, the churches, schools, council offices and the shops. Princess Road and Alexandra Road became

10 "The Welfare of the Needy by C Francis p27

important shopping centres where one could buy almost anything. There were also many corner shops where the daily needs of the local people were catered for.

The much-loved Denmark Road market too was a busy scene of shopping activity which we shall explore in a later chapter.

In 1894, Moss Side achieved Urban District Council status. This gave the Council wider powers to develop works of benefit to the local people. A Free Library was established next to the Council Offices, the Fire Station and Police Station were built just round the corner on Moss Lane East, handsome buildings, which would continue to serve their useful functions for many years until their demolition in the 1960's.

There were many changes still to come, in fact the story of Moss-Side is one of ongoing change. Change in its boundaries, change in its governing body, change from being a rural farming area to becoming a thriving suburb of the great City of Manchester, but, as we said at the start of this chapter, one thing has remained constant. The strength and pride of its inhabitants and their story deserves to be told.

Chapter 3

A Change of Government.

The Overseers who met at the "Waggon and Horses" pub, Longsight in 1835 to discuss setting the ley or rates for Moss Side, also set the pattern of sensible leadership by caring, responsible councilors, who always kept the welfare of their people in mind when making their decisions.

Important works, road building, housing, transport, health and safety were tackled urgently, successfully and in the best economic way, so keeping rates low. The people of Moss Side were happy with their council.

On 23rd June, 1856, the District of Moss Side Local Board of Health was formed, confirming a Provisional Order of the General Board of Health, under the Public Health Act, 1848.[11]

The people of Moss Side, then a very small population of 943 people, living in 153 houses, continued to live happily with their Local Board of Health, a new name, with probably the same caring councilors who continued to make decisions in the best interests of their people.

The second half of the 19th century saw a more rapid growth in the population of Moss Side. Many of the better paid, white collar workers employed in the offices, shops and warehouses of central Manchester were attracted to move to the cleaner air and well-built houses of Moss Side. By 1889 there were 24,100 people living in 4,820 houses paying rates to the Moss Side Local Board of Health.

As we have seen in the previous chapter, Moss Side council took advantage of changes in local government structure to become an Urban District Council. This gave the Council greater powers to raise loans for carrying out works for public purposes.

In 1892 Moss Lane was widened, in 1895 Alexandra Rd. was paved. 1899 saw the formation of Denmark Rd., work on the Raby St. sewer, improvement to Cornbrook St. and work on Tramways with the help of these loans.[12]

11 Moss Side Local Board publication Health Act, 1848. February 1890
12 Moss Side Local Board publication p4 Feb

These were important issues which enabled the new residents of Moss Side to commute from their homes to their place of work in the centre of the booming cotton industry of Manchester. There were further loans for expansion of Tramways and for widening Moss Lane East in 1901.

Because of the expansion of the tramway system a new depot was built on Princess Road and this was used for the first time on 10[th] July, 1909, although construction work was not complete.[13]

Many will remember it as the Bus Depot, which it became in 1939 when it was closed to trams.[14]

When the proposal for Moss Side to amalgamate with Manchester Council was announced in the late 1890's, it was welcomed mainly by the new residents, but was viewed with distrust by the original inhabitants who saw no benefit in becoming a small part of the powerful Manchester Council. They feared that rates would rise, that the interests and needs of Moss Side residents would not be recognized as had been the case with their own Urban District Council, and most of all they regretted and feared their loss of independence. All these issues were fiercely debated. Many meetings were held chaired by supporters for or against amalgamation.

Eventually the decision was reached by the vote. Each Moss Side resident was allowed one vote and the amalgamation with Manchester Council became official in October 1904.

Now that Moss Side had become part of Manchester, the dire warnings seem to have been largely forgotten. The area retained many of its own facilities such as the fire station and the library. There was some increase in the rates, but business continued to flourish and even expand.

As had always been the case, the population adapted, were proud of their area and welcomed new ideas and residents, more recently many from the West Indies, giving Moss Side of the late 20[th] century its own unique and happy character.

13 'Manchester's Little Train,' A.K. Kirby P13
14 'M/C Little Tram' p30

Me and my brother Trevor in the backyard in Fernleaf St
Moss Side in 1948

The last remaining view of Fernleaf St as most of the street has been demolished (in the 1960's slum clearance)
This picture was taken in 2018.

Chapter 4

The only address my mum had in Manchester, was in Moss Side where her brother-in-laws mother, Rose Wilson, lived. Rose lived in a small terraced house and we stayed with her, short term, in Ridley Grove, until we moved to another address in Fernleaf St (off Denmark Road). This house was much bigger and we rented 2 rooms at the top of the house. Mr. McPhilips who owned the house lived downstairs and had a television set in the front room. I remember him watching the 1948 Olympic Games which was held in London, but we were ushered out of this room when coverage of the Olympics were on. He had a very gruff Scottish voice and didn't seem very child friendly. I was only 2 years old and my brother Trevor was 3 years old so I imagine we could have been a bit of a handful to deal with. There was a small garden at the front of the house and we often played there. Many years later, I recall seeing Mr. McPhilips as a lolly-pop man looking after the zebra-crossing on Greenheys Lane/Denmark Rd corner by Quinxes Paper Shop. That was probably in 1958.

I only have a few memories concerning life in Fernleaf St but there was an incident of trying to find my Easter Eggs which had been hidden. I did not see the funny side of not being able to find mine, especially as my brother had found his and was happily munching away on them. I went into melt-down until dad eventually helped me to find them.

I remember the lay out of the house. We would walk in from the front door along a wide hallway and go up a wide staircase, turning left, the banister took us up another couple of steps to our living room which was at the end of a short passageway. This short passageway was always dark and I was always glad to get inside our living quarters. The living room had a big window which looked out onto Fernleaf St with a view of Seaton Street straight ahead.

Dad found a job working for British Railways near Piccadilly Train Station, driving a triangular type cab vehicle with a long trailer behind it. (This vehicle was called a Scammell Scarab).

The day we moved out of Fernleaf St. I remember looking at the empty room which had been home for a while.

Looking over in the corner of the room, there were lots of boxes which had been stacked in readiness for going to our new home in Wythenshawe. My dad came home with his British Rail vehicle and on the trailer was a brand new 3 piece suite. This was a present from "Horricks" where my mum worked. We loaded all the boxes up and set off for Staithes Road in Woodhouse Park, Wythenshawe. When we arrived at Staithes Rd. my brother had the task of choosing which house we were going to live in, as the houses were built but not yet occupied. He chose number 64. It was now August 1950.

Most of the houses in our new road were still being built and I remember there was a pond on the other side of the road from us, on the far right-hand side. It was quite dangerous and was later drained and filled in.

I was still very young and can only remember a few things of my Wythenshawe days but I do recall that when we had moved from Belgium to Moss Side, mum and dad had made friends with another couple, who were also coming from Belgium to Moss Side.

They had moved into their house in St Bee's St, which was only a couple of streets away from Fernleaf St. and they would regularly meet up with them. They had a young family which was good for my brother and I, as we could all play together.

Mr. and Mrs. King moved into their new home in Wythenshawe before we moved to Wythenshawe but we all still kept in touch. When we moved to Wythenshawe it was even easier to continue meeting up with them.

I do recall us all meeting up on a hot sunny day and we walked from our new Staithes Rd home to Manchester Airport (then known as Ringway). We took bottles of water with sherbert in it, and sandwiches as the airport was quite nearby. In those days, the airport was very basic, just a wire fence to separate you from the runway. There was an old shack which was where the passengers would wait before walking over to their plane. The shack was the only building which stood between people wanting to watch and people actually going on the plane to far off destinations. It was O-so-basic. To think how things have changed with security and the expansion of buildings and car parks etc nowadays.

Chapter 5

Woodhouse Park in Wythenshawe in about 1950 was being built up. It really was a big building site. There were no shops around us and only a small single-decker bus ran from Cornishway to Crossacres. From Crossacres you could catch a big double-decker bus to Manchester City Centre.

I remember walking across muddy fields from Staithes Rd to Cornishway, (where no houses had been built yet) and catching a bus to Northenden (via Crossacres) to my nursery, at a little church school (Now demolished and now where Tesco's Supermarket stands)

Mum would then walk back to Princess Parkway and catch another bus to her work in Cambridge St, near Dunlops Rubber Factory. She worked in a furniture warehouse/factory where she would sew leather coverings for chairs and settees.

Money was very tight and I remember her scrapping by each week. This arrangement could not last for long, so after a short period of time, mum and dad decided that all this travelling on buses to Manchester city centre was too expensive and made the decision to move back to Moss Side, where they could travel to their work more easily. We moved to a 2up/2down terraced house in Harrop St (which was later renamed Harlech St.

View taken in Harrop St
(Later Re-named Harlech St.)
Moss Side
Approx 1958.

Playing Cricket in the Street

2 more views of the Harlech St. Moss Side Approx 1958

Our house was the end house on the left

Chapter 6

I was now too old to be at Nursery School and the law said I had to go to a proper infant school when you are 5. Even though the house where we lived in Harrop St. was close by a junior school called Webster St School (about 200 yards away) I recall walking past this school to get to Princess Rd School which was about a mile away.

I recall going into a big office and meeting a scary headmaster called Mr. Cross. He accepted me and my real school - life started.

In those days Princess Rd School had a senior dept. for girls and boys up to the age of 15 years old, but when I moved out of the infants and into the juniors at the age of 7 (standard 1) the school became a primary school only and all the older children (over the age of 12) were moved out to secondary schools in the area.

The headmaster, Mr Cross retired shortly after I had moved upstairs to the juniors and a lady head-mistress called Miss Beven took up the helm. A few highlights in the news at about that time was Princess Grace of Monico marrage and the Queen's Coronation in 1953. A special set of postage stamps were issued by the post office for Princess Graces wedding and all the children in our class were encouraged to buy and keep these special stamps. The Queen's Coronation was also celebrated at school with a party and all the pupils received a Coronation Mug (a present from the Manchester Education Committee)

Another memory at that time were the awful prefects on the school entrance gates. School-life was quite harsh, as I remember trying to sneak into the playground in the mornings to avoid having my name taken for being late. One of the major rules was you had your name taken for being late and if you appeared on the late-list 3 times in a week; you were given the strap at Friday morning's assembly, in front of the whole school. Needless to say I was always border-line. Mr. Waller was the teacher to hand out the punishments and it was always as well to line up at the furthest end so that all the other children would take their punishment before you in the hope that Mr. Waller was getting tired.

At Princess Road School, there was a woodwork department housed in a separate part of the school which always fascinated me because older boys from senior schools used to come and have lessons with the resident carpenter teacher. We, as junior school pupils were never allowed to go into this room as the tools were far too dangerous for little fingers.

In the early days at Princess Rd School, I was still too young to go to school on my own so mum would take me and pick me up again later. We would quite often go to the park on Gt Western Street (known as the 'Rec') and sometimes as a special treat would go further down Princess Rd to Alexandra Park. Fishing for tidlers in the lake was always good fun as we would have to climb over a fence to get near the water. Every now and again a roar would go up that the Parky was coming and everyone would scamper back over the fence and run off. The "Parky," was always an old man, moving slowly, shouting and carrying a big walking stick. I don't think he ever caught anyone but he acted as a deterrent letting us know we shouldn't be over the fence.

Alexandra Park 1956 showing the lake and
Fence we used to climb over

Princess Rd Infants School in 1953

Picture taken at St James School Room which was on the corner of Gt. Western St/ Barnhill St.

The teacher was Miss Wilson

1953 Queen Elizabeth 2nd Coronation School Party at Princess Rd School

1954 - Princess Rd Class Picture. Mr Cross (Headmaster)
and Miss Derry were the teachers.

Chapter 7

As the years went by, my interest in football developed and one of the best days of my life was when I was picked to play in goals for the school team. I was a year younger than everyone else in the team as I was only in Standard 3. My brother was also in the team and most of his Standard 4 class friends made up the team. It wasn't a very good year for the team as they lost most of their games but the following year when our class moved up & became Standard 4, we won all our games and won the league. This was my last year at Princess Rd School and I always recall our sports teacher, Mr. Bradshaw getting the team together to discuss tactics and name the team for next Saturdays match. He would start off by naming the team and putting the initials of the team on the black-board starting with the goal-keeper, who was my best friend Bernard Thompson. It was always amusing to see B.T. go up first on the board as the M/c City goal-keeper at that time was Bert Trautmann and Mr. Bradshaw would always joke pointing out that Bert Trautmann wasn't playing for us this week. He had other commitments.

Picture of Bert Trautmann who broke his kneck whilst playing in the 1956
FA Cup Final at Wembley Stadium, for Manchester City
After recovering; he carried on playing for many years and retired in 1964.

Chapter 8

Whilst we were still at Princess Road Junior School, my brother and I joined St Clements Church choir and continued our interest in football (now outside the school environment)

We were not religious but St Clements were trying to get a football team together. The friends we made through joining the choir would remain with us forever. We had choir practices on Tuesday and Thursday nights and had a club social night on a Friday in a hall in Warwick St (which just along from the Linwood Pub.) Later we lost the use of this hall and transferred to Webster Street School for our Friday night club nights. We could listen to records or play table tennis, snooker, gymnastics or of course football. Football was always the main topic. Football was played on the roof at Webster St School (which was a little strange looking back) as this is where the playground was located. The roof was like a flat playground with a 5ft wall around it and a very sturdy fence on top of the wall. As you can imagine the playground was at the top of the school, very high up and occasionally the ball would be hit too high and over the fence.

It was a long way down to retrieve the ball, so the person who had kicked the ball over the fence would be forced to go down the stairs (and lots of them) to get the ball.

It gave everyone a break which was sometimes very welcome as every game was played like a cup-final with no holds barred. The game would resume as soon as the ball came back.

Although a great number of the St Clements Church Choir boys were now no longer choir boys due to their voices having broken, we still continued to go to the club evenings and play football.

The next stage was the formation of a proper team, and we joined a league which played on a Sunday.

At about this time I also joined the cubs at St. James Church on the corner of Princess Rd and Gt Western St. This brought me into conflict with each movement as both churches would have walks around the streets of Moss Side (whilst the Boys Brigade would supply the music) and I was expected to walk with the cubs and the choir. More often than not, these events would clash and I would have to make excuses to one or the other to keep the peace.

2 pictures of St Clements choir parading in Pigott St Moss Side 1956

St Clements Choir Football Team in its first season – 1957

St Clements Football Team 1961 with our 1st trophy
Photo taken on the roof at Webster St School

I enjoyed the Cubs Bob A Job Week which was usually held in the long school holidays in August. We rarely went on holiday in those days so the weeks passed by very slowly. Bob A Job Week usually lasted for about 2 weeks in my case as I used to find lots of customers & jobs to do. Denmark Road Market was a good source of income. I recall crushing boxes up for the stall holders. Alexandra Road with all their shops was another good place to find jobs. Shop-keepers were not the tidest of people and the cellers were usually filled with all sorts of packaging and boxes. Sweeping and tidying up were usually the order of the day. Little old ladies liked to have their dogs walked and on one occasion, I had to climb a tree to rescue a cat. Taking empty pop bottles back to the shop and collecting the deposit off the bottles was particularly good as I gained the 2d and they usually paid for the convenience of clearing the bottles out of the way.

I recall representing our cub-pack in a sports day event in Birchfield Park where by lots of Cub Packs had sent a team to compete for the Manchester Cubs Sheild. Our St James Pack won the event, which we had never done before. I contributed to our points total by winning 5 events and coming 3rd in the 3 legged race.

Chapter 9

There seemed to be 3 major shopping streets which we used to visit on many occassions. These were Stretford Rd, Princess Rd and Alexandra Rd. Depending on which direction you went in, you could buy practically anything.

The Sports Depot on Princess Rd was my favourate shop. They had model trains and planes in one part of the shop and tennis rackets and sports equipment and clothing, footballs, model-farms, toy cars and they even had a joke section in another part of the shop.

Next door to the Sports Depot was Thorntons Chocolate Cabin where my brother and I were allowed to spend 6d on chocolate, as a Friday night treat, on our way home from school.

If we walked from our house in the direction of Jackson St, it was usually because we were going to Woolworths which was on the corner of Stretford Rd and Jackson St. Stretford Rd was a very long road with lots of individual shops on either side of the road and went all the way up from Woolworths to Pauldens. Pauldens was a big departmental store on Cambridge St. until 1957 when it was burnt down. I recall going to Pauldens the day before it burnt down to get my new school uniform as I was going to start at Yew Tree School in Wythenshawe the following week. Mum and Dad took us to see the blaze which was quite horrific. The firemen just didn't seem to be able to get control of the situation. The site remained derelict for years after, never recovering from the disaster.

Alexandra Rd. was again a long road with lots of individual shops on either side of the road and ran from Moss Lane East, past Great Western St and continued all the way up to Alexandra Park. I always seemed to get my shoes from BATA on Alexandra Rd and I recall buying my 1st and 2nd records from Woolworth, also on Alexandra Rd. Dad had gone and bought a new record player so we now needed to get some records to play on it.

It was 1957 and the 2 records we bought were "Diana" by Paul Anker and "Last Train to San Fernando" by Johnny Duncan. The records were 78's, heavy and easily broken. They were played continuously until the inevitable happened and they ended up being broken and binned.

Moss Side - Manchester

1950's / 1960's

Nostalgic Memories.

Picture taken from Men Newspaper in the 60's

Taken July 1997

2 photographs taken from Alexandra Park Gates on Alexandra Road, Moss Side
All the shops have gone and been replaced by houses. Only the church at the
far end has survived and the post box on the left hand side.

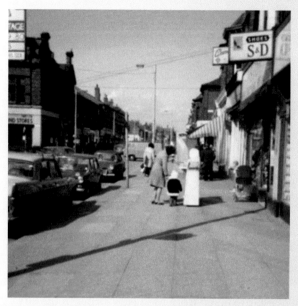

A view looking down Alexandra Road in 1973 when Alexandra Road was a main shopping area.

The same view taken in 2018

Chapter 10

I used to go to the baths to learn to swim with Princess Rd School but for some reason, I could never get the hang of it. Most of my classmates would be splashing about and having a great time but I would hang onto the side of the wall, hating every minute of the lesson. We used to go to Broadfield Road Swimming Baths which was an old Victorian baths near the Bus Depot. Our school used to have inter-schools gala's which I never took part in as I couldn't swim. These Gala's were held at Victoria Baths on Hathersage Road. We used to go along to support our school and occasionally went to this venue for our school swimming lessons. (Just for the record, I did eventually learn to swim when I was 23 yrs old and looked back on all the fun I had missed out on).

Another sport I got into when I was about 12 yrs old; was tennis. I had a school-friend called Melvin and we would go to Alexandra Park and play for hours. We became quite good and I remember Melvins mum saying we should take it up and enter some competitions. This never happened but I still love watching the big tennis tournaments, especially Wimbledon,

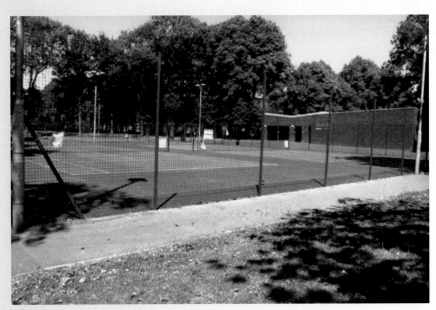

The tennis courts at Alexandra Park.

Chapter 11

I used to have my haircut at a barbers on Embden St. He was a very sociable hairdresser who would put a piece of wood across the two arms of the chair for small children to sit on to raise them up to a higher level. There were always comic's to be read and at the end of your haircut he would let you pick a raffle ticket out of his box. You always won a prize of some sort of sweets; needless to say I liked to go for my haircut there. Embden St was not a major shopping street but it did have a good collection of shops. There was a Chemist, a toyshop a hardware shop, a Post Office, a butchers and greengrocers, and I was sent on errands on many occasions to bring back bits & pieces.

My paper-round was around this area and I recall becoming a bookies-runner for an old gentleman who lived in College St. I would call on him every night as he was housebound and he would give me his bet on a slip of paper and the stake, plus my three penny tip and off I would go to a back yard near Vine St. The following night I would do the same trip and pick up any winnings he had won. As betting was illegal in those days and betting shops had not yet been established, I had to be careful not to attract too much attention when approaching this back yard. I'm sure the police must have turned a blind eye to the goings on around, as the entries were always busy around there. I was quite surprised to find a few years later that new laws had come in and betting shops began appearing on our streets. My life of crime was over but I had found it an exciting experience helping a housebound old gentleman; giving him a little pleasure in life.

Chapter 12-Our House.

The house we lived in from 1951 to 1967 was a 2 up-2 down, terraced house. There was a small kitchen, a small back yard and an outside loo. Upstairs my brother and I shared the big bedroom, whilest mum and dad had the smaller bedroom. Most of the houses in our area were more or less the same and I can only imagine that conditions inside the houses were similar to ours. We had no bathroom or central heating and no running hot water. The hot water was produced by a geysor or a kettle boiled on the gas cooker. There were fireplaces in both of the downstairs rooms but the front room fireplace was rarely used as we kept this room tidy in case we had visitors. The living room fireplace was in constant use in the winter, being lit every morning with paper and wood and coal thrown on top. The kitchen floor was a stone floor similar to the back yard and pavements outside in the streets. The windows were sash windows and only had a single pane of glass in them. No such thing as double-glazing. In winter, ice would form on the inside of the windows. The house was always cold and damp.

We also had a cellar which was where the coal was kept and we also had a bath in the cellar. Next to the bath was a boiler which dad would fill with cold water and light the gas jets underneath. When the water was hot enough, he would pan out the hot water into the bath and call us. It was our weekly bath time. Normal daily washes were carried out in the kitchen sink.

Looking back I recall how bad the condition of the building was. Many a night was spent in bed with buckets underneath a leaky roof, listening to the drips falling down from the ceiling. We were not allowed to switch the light on, on many occasions as it would cause the lights to fuse. Whenever the rain leaked in, mum would have to ring up the landlord and he would send the builder round to repair the roof. This was quite a common occurrence as the job never seemed to be done properly.

The plaster on the walls were in a bad state; very crumbly and it was only the wallpaper which held the plaster from completely falling off the wall.

I remember dad taking the wallpaper off the wall in the hallway when he decided to decorate and big chunks of plaster would fall off. Dad would go and get some new packets of plaster from the hardware store on Emden St and skim the walls and then wait for days whilst the plaster dried out, before he could continue with the decorating.

All the floors in all the rooms were covered with lino.- No carpets in those days for us.

Our house was on the corner of Crowborough St and Harlech St and was back to back with the Pineapple Public House. Only a back entry separated our house from the pub.

You can just see our house on the right hand side (just beyond the pub)

The pub was at one time owned by my gran Rose Wilson who we mentioned in Introduction No. 2. Rose moved from the Pineapple Pub to Ridley Grove in the 1940's

After the demolition of the Pinapple Pub and our old house - I have traced the exact spot where these building stood. (On the new estate)
On the corner of Bronte St/Aquarius St.

Chapter 13

There were quite a few local corner shops in our area. Our nearest corner shop was Skelhorns which was on the corner of Leaf St (later renamed as Crowborough St) and Ridley Grove. Skelhorns would allow credit to good paying customers and although the shop was only small, it was always crowded. You could get all sorts of groceries or so it seemed. I recall my mother used to make out a weekly shopping list of items she wanted on Friday evening and put an "X" against items which she wanted immediately. The list was handed to Skelhorns shop on a Tuesday and as the week progressed; I would go in on Wednesday and Thursday and have an X put against certain items which were needed before Friday evening and bring them home early. On Friday night I would pick up the balance of the order and pay the bill. It was always paid in cash as mum and dad received their wages from work (in cash) on a Friday evening.

A view of our cat on our back yard wall looking down Crowborough St. Lucknow Grove is to the right. The next road down is Ridley Grove and you can just see the Butchers and Skelhorns Shop on each of the corners.

Skelhorns Shop was really good for the community around, as each year, they would hire a coach and take all the local children on a bus trip to Pickmere Lake, which was out in the country near Knutsford, Cheshire. They would

supply all the children with sweets and drinks and give them a really good fun time. At Pickmere there was a small amusement park and rowing boats were in constant use on the lake.

This was the view we had when we stepped out from our front door. (Harlech St)
Looking down Crowborough St at Skelhorns Shop and the Butchers in Ridley Grove

Chapter 14

It was a big day for my brother Trevor when he sat the 11 plus exam and passed for Grammer School. He went to Chorlton Grammer. He was rewarded with £5 from Aunty Lucy who had made a flying visit from abroad to stay with her mother-in-law in Ridley Grove, and see my mum (her sister). Aunty Lucy said I had to fetch my school report for her to see and luckily the report wasn't too bad. I say luckily because I was also rewarded with £5. This money was wonderful because the following weekend I was going on our annual choir camp in Holywell, North Wales and I would have lots of spending money to take with me.

Eventually it was my turn to take the 11 plus exam and I went along to Heald Place School with my pen and ruler to sit the exam. When the results came out, I was given a place at Yew Tree Comprehensive School in Wythenshawe. This school was given the title of Comprehensive School and was an experimental forerunner of a school sitting between secondary and Grammer School but in 1957/58, it was still experimental. In later years it became commonplace to see schools changing to Comprehensive Schools. Yew Tree was a very big school of its time with 1200 pupils with compulsory 1-4 years and an optional 5th year for pupils to take GCE's etc. and even had a 6th year if pupils wanted to stay on to take 'A' levels. I wasn't a very good student as my homework was done in a rush and handed in late because I had to go out most evenings to the Rec or Alexandra Park to play football or tennis. (Sports were highest on my agenda in those days.)

Youth Clubs were the next sauce of interest to me and I joined a number of these clubs, generally run by schools. Princess Rd School had a youth club and we started to go to play and listen to records. We also joined the youth club at Old Moat School, where we could play table-tennis, darts, snooker etc. I used to go to these clubs with 2 main friends called Alan Jeffs and Malcolm G. who lived in the next streets to me. We met through being in St Clements Choir.

St Clements Church on Greenheys Lane opposite Denmark Road Market

Our house was near Denmark Road Market and quite often I would go along to see if I could earn some pocket money, cleaning cars or working on the stalls. The market which was positioned on Greenheys Lane, between St Clements Church and Webster St School was always a hive of activity. There were lots of fruit & veg stalls and a lady used to sell 2nd-hand clothes. There was a lino stall whereby 2 men would roll out the lino on the ground and cut off whatever length the customer required. There was a biscuit stall where I recall mum, quite often bought a bag of broken biscuits at a very much reduced price. Just outside the market on a corner, surrounded by houses, there was a cafe with sticky tables and floors and smelt pretty awful, but always seemed very popular.

We lived near enough to Maine Road (Home Ground of Manchester City F.C) and could walk there to see City play. We were able to get free tickets from school to watch the City reserves play in the Central League but had to pay school-boy prices to watch City's 1st Team games. (I think school-boy prices were 1 shilling and three pence) Luckily I had a paper-round to give me enough money to do everything I wanted to do. On Saturday's I had to collect the paper-money from the customers on my round and the tips I got, also helped.

On the left is the fencing which went around Denmark Rd Market on Greenheys Lane. The 3rd shop along from the market was Quinxes Paper Shop.

Washing cars outside Denmark Rd Market

Me in our street (Harlech St. Moss Side) with Lucknow Grove in the background. (Aprox 1961)

Years later - taken from our house looking down Lucknow Grove.

Chapter 15

From Harrop St (Later re-named Harlech St) we were well served by cinema's as we had the Wycliffe, the Cresent, the College and the Poplar, all within a few hundred yards, but slowly but surely these cinemas were taken over as Bingo Halls which had become very popular. Even the Hulme Hippodrone which used to stage variety performances was taken over by the Bingo craze.

There always seemed to be a hive of activity just outside our front door as we were not far away from the coal-yard in Piggot St. Ladies would fill up there old prams with coal or coke and wheel them home. Cars were not everywhere like they are today and carrying items in old prams were quite common. Tradesmen used hand carts as cars and vans were difficult to get and were very expensive. Even the rag-and-bone man had a big cart, pulled by a horse. By giving him something to put on his cart; you were rewarded with either a bow-and-arrow or a gold fish. You were lucky if the gold fish managed to survive for a week, but some did.

It was the days of the Corona-man who fetched the Pop (mineral) and the paper-man who came along the streets, shouting 'Football Pink' on a Saturday evening. Anyone who had not heard the football results on the 5 pm radio results program (which still exists today) would be rushing out to get their copy of the Sports Football Pink, so they could check their football coupons, in the hope of winning a fortune. Of course we had the ice-cream man calling around, ringing a hand-bell to attract his customers. We even had a Rowlands bread-man, a Greengrocers man and a Milk-man. The Co-Op milk-man used to call round on a Saturday morning for his money and I would sometimes have to go to the door to pay him. He would always ask for our Co-Op number which I still remember to this day (118323)

Mum would get a dividend at the end of the year as a payback for being a good customer.

Saturday was just a constant procession of callers coming for their payments. (Papers, bread, lemonade, window-cleaner, Insurance Man, Coal-man) The rent money was always passed to Mrs. Kelly who lived at No 9, on a Monday morning, as this was the day the landlord called.

Mrs. Kelly was a real old battle-axe who knew everyone's business or so it seemed. She was the original "Every street has got one." I'm sure she was alright really as she had most people's keys in the street and that was very useful considering how many times we found ourselves locked out. When the meter-reader called to read the meters for Gas & Electric, it was Mrs. Kelly who would let them in. Meter reading days were always good, because after the meters were read and emptied of all the shillings, the meter man would balance up and give mum some of the

money back. Moss Side was a constant procession of people moving around delivering or selling. When you look at the layout of rows and rows of terraced house's with no gardens or very small gardens, door to door knocking or making deliveries; must have been so easy to do, compared to the suburban type semi-detached or detached estates with large gardens which now exist.

Children would play in the streets and seasonal games and activities would come around every year. Hop-scotch, swinging round the lamp-posts, marbles, Yo-Yo's, Conkers to name a few. At Christmas time there were lots of decorations to be made. Paper-chains were always popular and at school there were always very bright squares of gummed paper which were just the right size for cutting into strips and looping through to make the perfect paper-chain. At home, I would make them out of crape paper & glue made from flour & water.

Household items used to last much longer as they were made of a more substantial material than they are made from today. We have definitely become a nation of use, break and throw away and replace whereas years ago we would go to great lengths to have repaired.

Cobblers could be found in all areas and were a necessary tradesman. Shoes have always been expensive and having shoes repaired was a normal thing to have done. Tailor shops could be found in great numbers where you would choose your cloth and colour from sample books and be measured up for a suit. When the suit had been made, you would go for a fitting and any adjustments needed would be done before you took the suit away and started paying for it, on a weekly basis. Nowadays, High St. off the peg and Sports-gear seem to be main outlets for clothes (Not to mention Catalouge Shopping). Catalogue Shopping has always been around as I recall hunting through my parents Littlewoods or John Myers Catalogue for Christmas presents. Somehow they never actually seemed as good as they looked in the catalogue, when the items arrived. Most early plastic products were very brittle and cracked easily.

The Hulme Hippodrome which used to host variety shows but later became a Bingo Hall before closing altogether. (view taken in 1997)

Chapter 16

There always seemed more of a community spirit about Moss Side in the fifties and sixties. Maybe it was because of the small terraced housing which existed and people were closer to each other. The feeling generally of helping each other because times were hard and the 2nd World War was still very fresh in everyone's mind. There had been a great lack of materialistic things around and as time moved on, manufacturers were having a good time with new inventions, marketing and generally attempting to show ordinary people that they could own this and that and be one step ahead. The expression of "Keeping up with the Jones's" was a statement put out by manufacturers, to encourage people buy their products.

Bon-Fire nights were always exiting for the children. My brother & I used to collect one firework each night on our way home from school, for weeks before Bon-Fire night. We usually went to the Post Office on Embden St as they always had a good selection to pick from, and it was amazing how our collection would grow.

In the late fifties and early sixties the streets were still cobbled and we would build the bon-fires in the middle of the street. It was common-place to have bon-fires in most streets. The children would be out for weeks before bon-fire night, collecting wood & burnable items and would store them in the cellars or back-yards.

It was good to see the building of the bon-fires on the actual night as cellers and back-yards were slowly emptied out. Sometimes the fires were built too large and as you can imagine, this would cause a problem later when the fire was lit, creating a hazard as the fires would be too close to the houses and the fire brigade were constantly being called out. They had further problems getting to the fires as they had to maneuver around other streets with fires burning.

The cobbled streets were later tarred and stone chippings laid on the tar at which point, bon-fires were no longer allowed in the streets. The bon-fires were moved onto the many cinder-crofts which existed in the area. (Due to houses being bombed in the war)

Chapter 17

Days out from Moss Side

Although we very rarely went away on holidays, we did have lots of days out to different places when mum and dad bought a car. It was an old Austin 10, black and very unreliable. I'm not sure of the year it was bought but I will hazard a guess that it was probably about 1954: but I certainly do remember the car spending lots of time in the garage being repaired.

It was just nice to be able to come home from school, have our tea and dad to announce we were going out to Wythenshawe Park or somewhere fairly local to us. Wythenshawe Park was probably only about 3 or 4 miles away but it seemed like another world. We would gather up a football and fishing nets and set off for what seemed like a trip into the country.

Another venue I recall going to on a number of occasions was a trip to Knutsford. Dad who worked for British Railways, made deliveries from a railway station in Manchester, to a number of farms out in the country. Knutsford was a popular run for him and he would quite often come home at night with a bag full of apples or a tray of eggs or even a selection of vegetables which the farms had given to dad. Consequently he got to know Knutsford quite well so as a treat for us, he would take us in the car to places he had discovered. I know he quite often made deliveries to Joddral Bank with new parts for the giant telescope which was being built at Holmes Chapel. Again there were lots of farms around and again he would come home with lots of nice things. He could never take us to the Joddral Bank site as it was a working site and not a place for visitors, as it is today.

Castle Mills was also a popular destination when we were younger. We would park the car up on the road and walk down a pathway, over a style and into a big field. At the end of the field was the River Bollin where we could swim (or in my case paddle). There was a big open-air swimming pool and café on the other side of the road but this was demolished later. I think that was due to a serious accident. Another day out in roughly the same area as Castle Mills was Styal Woods. This was a heavily wooded area which also had the River Bollin running through it. Once you had walked through the woods on its rickety footpaths, you came across an old mill and lots of old houses which apparently the workers at the mill used to live in.

A trip to see the lights at Blackpool was always special. The only problem was the traffic. It was in the days before motorways had been built and we had to travel on country type lanes to get there. It took forever but it was magical when we did arrive. We could play on the sands, eat fish and chips and buy a stick of Blackpool rock. Then we wait for it to go dark. Everyone would que up in their cars and at the appointed time, the marshals would let the cars go. It wasn't a race, it was a leisurely drive through a wonderful themed set of coloured lights that went on for miles.

Mum and dad eventually disposed of car, as it became a liability when it got to the stage of not knowing if the brakes would work properly or if the car would make it up the next hill.

They then bought a Lambretta Scooter which would keep them mobile and I can still picture them now travelling up Princess Road to their newly acquired allotment which was situated between Hough End Sports Field and Southern Cemetery. They spent many years tending to their crops and became very good growers of veggies and potatoes etc. My brother and I were also brought into the gardening fun as we were both given a little plot of land to grow anything we wanted. I think that is when we realised that mum and dad had green fingers, but our fingers were of a different colour as we never really grew anything other than weeds.

Mum and Dad's allotment.

Visits to Belle Vue Zoo were quite common to our family in the early sixties as we were not too far away from the zoo and mum always considered it to be both educational and a good day out. We would walk to Lloyd Street (which was near the Dental Hospital) and take a short bus ride on the No. 53 bus to the zoo.

Although I say it was quite common for us to go there, as kids we didn't realize that there must have been quite an expense attached to this particular day out.

I was always interested in the massive tortoise which all the little children could queue up for and have a ride on its back. This was later stopped as it was thought to be a little on the cruel side.

The monkeys were always lively, playing and having fun. They had all the animals you would expect to see at the zoo such as Lions, Tigers, Hippos, Giraffes, Zebras, Elephants, Cattle, Camels, Wolves, and a whole array of different types of birds (large and small). There were many ponds with all sorts of water type animals in them and a black bear pit. There was even a pool where Polar Bears could walk and swim around. There were lots of separate building which housed fish and reptiles.

You could even take a ride on the back of an elephant. A specially adapted seat which sat on the elephants back was filled up with 4 or 5 small children and off you would go. You could also take a trip in a horse and cart around the site and there was a mini-railway.

Later on, many changes were made to the zoo as more and more out buildings were erected as shows and catering were introduced and the zoo began being run down. The fun-fair side of things started to take over and many functions began taking place.

The last of the animals to be moved out was an elephant called "Ellie May" in February 1979. A new home had been found for the elephant but when the staff attempted to transfer her to the transport, she refused to leave. Overnight Ellie May developed pneumonia and a serious heart complaint and they decided that it would be a kindness to have her put down.

Boxing and wrestling bouts began taking place and Speedway (Motor-cycle racing,) Stock-car racing were also very popular events. Conferences and musical shows, dances, football, athletics were all staged at Belle Vue. The animals were slowly being moved out to other zoos in other parts of the world. The fun-fair was expanding and became the main attraction. There always seemed to be a circus on around Christmas time and I recall going to the circus with Princes Road School as a special treat. The audiences were made up of lots of children from lots of different schools. I also remember representing Princess Road School on the sports field at Belle Vue running in the 100 yards race and the 4 x 100 yards relay against other schools from the Manchester area. I used to think I was quite a fast runner until that Sports Day when I was well and truly put in my place, by finishing well down in the finishing places.

It would seem that Belle Vue as a zoo and entertainment centre could not keep pace with other zoos close to Manchester and after struggling on for a number of years; piece by piece, the buildings were being taken down, until finally in 1986, the last building was demolished and the land was taken over by a firm who ran a car auction.

Chapter 18

As my brother & I were now that bit older and beginning to fend for ourselves, my mum took the opportunity to go to evening classes at a college in Manchester to retake all the exams which she needed, to get into Teacher Training College; as she still had the ambition to become a teacher. She was now 35 years old, and she passed all the qualifications she needed in a single year.

Then it was off to Teacher Training College for 3 years. Times were hard as we now only had dad working and his wages had to cover all our expenses. It was a proud moment for all of us, when mum finally passed out to become a qualified teacher. She had finally achieved her ambition. She loved her job and continued to teach for the next 30 years; continuing for years after her retirement age, as she felt she had missed out at the beginning of her career.

Odds bits of memories

Although my dad liked to have a drink of beer, he rarely went into pubs unless it was for a social event, in spite of the fact that the Pineapple Pub was directly at the back of our house. He preferred to have a drink in the house and to do this he would take some empty lemonade bottles to an off-licence shop on the corner of Brayshaw Street/Warwick Street, and the shop-keeper would fill up his bottles with dads preferred brand of beer.

Later on, he progressed to buying his beer in big cans called Party Fours or even bigger cans called Party Sevens. They were made by Watneys and came in a red and gold can.

After the 2nd World War had ended, a lot of the goods in the shops were still being rationed and I recall having to go to a hall in Great Western Street to pick up new ration books. Ration books had been introduced during the war in an attempt to ensure that everyone had a even chance of providing essentials for their families. Rationing carried on for several years after the war had ended but as certain items became more available and the shops began coping with peoples demands, these goods were taken off rationing. The ration books were scaled down and eventually stopped altogether.

Football has always been a high priority in my life and as I mentioned in earlier chapters (Manchester City have always been the team I have supported) possibly due to the location of the stadium being close to my home in Moss Side.

Manchester City moved from their Maine Road Stadium in 2003 to a new home (Now known as the Etihad Stadium). The old Maine Road Stadium was demolished and a new housing estate has been built on the cleared ground.

Before all trace of where the stadium used to be; the planners of the new housing estate had the foresight to mark exactly where the centre-spot of the old Maine Road football pitch was, and have now marked the spot with a commemorative stone. The new houses were then built around the commemorative and can be viewed by walking down Carnival Place off Billsborrow Road.

Saturday mornings were usually film mornings as most of the local cinemas used to run a children's film club whereby you could see Roy Rogers (Cowboy film) The Three Studies (Comedy), Cartoons and a serial which always ended with a cliff-hanging finish to encourage you to go next week to see how the story developed.

There used to be a theatre on Denmark Road and I remember going there with my brother and cousin Janet (who was staying with our Gran (Rose Wilson) for a while) and Gran had bought tickets for us all to go and see "Mr Pastry". Although the theatre was probably only a mile away, I recall Gran struggling to walk all the way there and we had to keep stopping to let her catch her breath. We did manage to make it there in time and enjoyed the show. The show was a rather silly slap-stick comedy but it appealed to most of the audience with lots of comical stunts involved.

The theatre building is still there today but has now been put to other uses (offices and businesses).

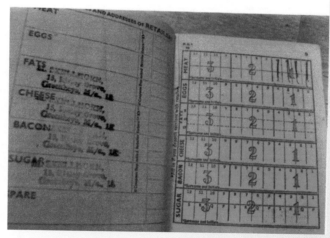

Ration Books were still in use in 1954

The Commemorative Stone which shows where the centre of the pitch was at the old Maine Road Stadium

The old theatre on Denmark Rd in Moss Side.

Chapter 19

Another part of my growing up years was a trip to a shop on Vine St off Embden St to buy a 2d Woody. (Woody was the nick-name for a Woodbine cigarette) which were normally sold in packets of 5's/10's and 20's. This particular shop would sell them individually at 2d a cigarette which was better for me as I was only learning how to smoke. It seemed that smoking was the thing to do in those days as most of my friends smoked and people were not really aware of the problems (health wise) smoking could cause, later in life.

I do recall, on one of these occasions of going to buy a 2d Woody that the conversation in the shop was about a new television program which was about to start called "Coronation Street." This must have been about 1960 and was on our screens in black and white with only 1 episode per week. The show became very popular and is still running to this day, in colour and is now on several times a week.

There are so many fleeting memories of life back in the 50's/60's. Nowadays we are attracted to specialist sweet shops which sell old fashion sweets but back in the day, it was quite normal to see packets of spangles, jars of flying saucers, sherbert, liquorish sticks and jelly beans in our corner shops. Most of their products have now disappeared from the shelves although some super-markets do still carry them in pre-packed bags. As rationing was still a concern, especially on sweets, everyone was limited as to what you could buy. It was normal to buy sweets in 2 oz's or 4 oz's bags. Even the bags were different in shape. The 2 oz bag was shaped like a cone whereas the 4 oz bags were square.

Whatever happened to Donkey Stones?

You could buy them in various colours and would see ladies with a bucket and cloth washing the front door step and scraping the donkey stone over the washed steps, then smoothing over with a damp cloth. This gave a nice welcoming effect to visitors calling but only lasted for a short length of time, as the effect some wore off when someone walked on the newly donkey-stoned step and left a footprint on it.

Chapter 20

Princess Road.

In an area with so much history, it is difficult to choose where to begin. However we must begin somewhere and it seems logical to choose this part of Moss Side, as it was here that the original Council Offices stood. Moss Side Library was on the corner of Moss Lane East and Princess Road.

The Police Station and Fire Station were just around the corner from the library. I recall the police station had horses at the back of the station and they always looked very smart and well groomed. My brother and I were both members of the children's library but reading books was never a pleasure to me.

Staying on the same side of Princess Road, going across Moss Lane East was a supermarket which later became the Nile Club. Incorporated in the Nile Club was another club called Reno and the Wycliffe Picture House, was next. Following up the road was a whole row of shops. Harrison's hardware shop, a sweet shop, jewallery shop to name a few until you reached Raby St. On the other side of Princess Road going up from Moss Lane East was the Alex Pub, Martins Bank, Thornton's Chocolate Cabin and the best shop in the world called "The Sports Depot." Mum bought me my very first pair of football boots from there when I was 8. The Sports Depot was quite a long shop and they had windows to display lots of their goods. One of the windows held second hand goods and that is where I spotted my football boots. They were red, high sided and had no studs in them. You had to buy studs separately and hammer them into the sole of the boot. I couldn't believe it when she took me into the shop and bought them for me. These boots went back to the same window a year later as my feet had outgrown them. Roy Clarke, who played for Man City at the time sometimes worked there. I always liked to go in there as they also sold spare pieces of Meccano at 1d each part. I loved to build things out of Meccano as a youngster and this shop would hold my attention for years. The Meccano pieces were held in a long wooden box and you could go through the box looking for special pieces.

Moving on up Princess Road going over a couple of smaller roads, you eventually arrived at Princess Road Primary School.

After the school, there were more shops and crossing over Great Western St, another endless stream of individual shops, one of which was Horners (the bike shop) where I got my first bike from. Horners were very accommodating

to their customers as I remember having the seat altered to allow the seat to sit lower in the bike frame, as my legs were not long enough to reach the pedals properly. I had to go back to the shop the next day to pick up my adjusted new bike when Mr. Horner had made a specially welded bracket for my seat.

Moving further up Princess Rd was my dentist (which I hated). The dentist was old school and didn't show much compassion for his patients.

The next road we came to was Claremont Rd and by turning right here, you could make your way into Alexandra Park. As you entered the park, there was a nursery school on the right hand side where little toddlers could be seen playing in their own outside little play area.

In the park, there were gardens and a large bowling green, a large circular field which had huge trees all around the perimeter of the field. There were tennis courts and a putting green and a big greenhouse with lots of exotic plants. By going past the big green house, you could make your way back out of the park, back onto Princess Rd. again.

Crossing over the road, you came to the Bus Depot, which was an enormous building, housing Manchester's buses overnight. Working your way back down Princess Rd in the direction of our starting point of Moss Lane East, there were lots more individual shops, houses, a church, under-takers and supermarkets.

The Bus Depot on Princess Rd. Moss Side.

Chapter 21

My Old Library Ticket

Ticket expires___ **APR 1964**

Mr. A. WILLIAMS
1 Harlech Street
Greenheys, M/C. 15

**MANCHESTER
PUBLIC LIBRARIES**

This Ticket may be used at
any of the Libraries but is
not transferable.
Change of address must be
notified without delay.

AVAILABLE FOR ALL BOOKS
MOSS SIDE L641

Moss Side Library which was opened in 1896

Princess Road School on Princess Road Moss Side

The Sundial which was on the wall at Princess Rd School (on Princess Rd) was later re-erected on the wall at the new Princess Rd School on Alexandra Rd

Re-erected on the wall at the New Princess Rd School on Alexandra Rd

Princess Rd School on Alexandra Rd

City of Manchester

City Architect's Department
P O Box 488
Town Hall
Manchester M60 2JT
Telephone 061-236 3377

S A B Heppell BA RIBA DIP TP
City Architect

Your reference
Our reference BS/FP/AD
Date 12th June 1975

If telephoning or calling please
ask for Mr. Pearson
extension 2274

Dear Sirs,

Princess Road Primary School
Princess Road, Moss Side.

Further to your letter regarding the sun dial and
motto on the side wall of the school, I would inform you that
it is the City Council's intention to incorporate this in the
new Princess Road Primary School which is at the present being
erected in Alexandra Road, Moss Side.

Yours faithfully,

S. A. B. Heppell

City Architect.

Mum was interested in purchasing the Sun Dial which was on the wall at the old Princess Road School and wrote to the City Architect's Dept to see if this could be arranged. But the reply came back saying that when the old school was demolished, the sun-dial would be built into the wall of the new Princess Road School on Alexandra Road. The reply letter is above.

The Tree Line on the left is where Princess Road School used to be. The bus stop on the R.H. Side is in the same position as it was before the school was demolished. Picture taken from Gt. Western St end looking towards Raby St. (2018)

The Greenhouse in Alexandra Park, Moss Side (now demolished)

The Bowling Green in Alexandra Park.

The Drinking Fountain in Alexandra Park

The lake in Alexandra Park

Chapter 22

A Few Famous People from Moss Side

There have been lots of famous people who have come from Moss Side and I feel it is only correct to mention a few of these people.

Anthony Burgess 1917-1993 - who wrote A Clockwork Orange was born in Harpurhey in Manchester. He moved to a tobacconist shop in Princess Road and lived in a fantasy world of his own, according to Roger Lewis (who was Burgess's biographer).

He appeared on television with Michael Parkinson and Terry Wogan telling of how he only had a year to live due to a brain tumour and so he had written five novels in a year, in 1959. It was later discovered that these books had been written over a period of 15 to 20 years and the publishers had rejected these works. They were later found in a drawer on yellowing paper. He eventually died of lung cancer in 1993 in a London hospital.

Charles Halle 1819-1895 - The famous orchestra leader was born in Hagen, Germany. He moved to Paris, then London before settling down in Victoria Park (Addison Terrace) Manchester. He then moved to Duxbury Square in Moss Side. He had arrived in Manchester with the task of putting together a small orchestra in 1857 to play for Prince Albert at the opening ceremony to an exhibition called "Art Treasures of Great Britain" which was the biggest single exhibition Manchester had ever staged. Later his orchestra took up residency at the Free Trade Hall. He was knighted in 1888 which was the same year as he married his second wife, Madame Norman Neruda, who herself, was a famous violinist.

There is now a road in Moss Side named after him, just off Denmark Road. He died at his home at 70, Greenheys Lane, in 1895 (Now demolished)

Elizabeth Gaskell 1810-1865- was born in Chelsea, London and wrote many books. Her most famous books were Mary Barton, Cranford and North and South. After her mother died in 1811, she was brought up by her aunt Hannah Lumb in Knutsford, Cheshire. In 1832 she married William Gaskell and settled in Victoria Park, Manchester, before

moving to Plymouth Grove in 1850 (which was only a short distance from Victoria Park). Her house in Plymouth Grove is now open to the public. She became friends with Charles Dickens and Charlotte Bronte

She died of a heart attack in 1865 and was buried in Brook St Unitarian Chaple in Knutsford. Her husband William who was a Unitarian Minister survived Elizabeth by almost 20 years passing away in 1884.

Emily Pankhurst (nee Goulden) 1858-1928.

Emily grew up in Moss Side, Manchester and married Richard Pankhurst in 1879. Richard was a lawyer and supporter of women's sufferage movement. He was also a member of Parliment and wrote the married Womens Property Act of 1870. Emily and Richard moved to London in 1885 to continue their struggle for women's rights. In 1893 they returned back to Manchester but Richard who was suffering with gastric ulcers, eventually passed away in 1898. He was buried at Brooklands Cemetery with lots of dignitaries attending the funeral. Emily Pankhurst continued the fight, campaigning for women to be given the right to vote. At her home at 62 Nelson St, the suffragette movement was born when she invited a number of women into her front room in October 1903 with the sole purpose of forming an organization known as the Women's Social and Political Union (W.S.P.U) Plans were put in place to cause as much disruption as possible so that the politicians of the day would listen to women's demands. They protested by smashing windows, arson and going on hunger strikes in prison. In 1913, Emily Davidson, who was a member of the W.S.P.U. was killed when she stepped out in front of the kings horse at the Derby horse race, in protest at the government's failure to grant women the vote. In 1918 women over the age of 30 were given the vote and in 1928 women were given the same rights as men. Emily Pankhurst died soon after in 1928. Today a museum exists at Emily Pankhurst's old house at 62, Nelson St, Manchester. The house had fallen into a very poor state; but a group of supporters felt the house should be saved and set about restoring the building. This is still going on and great advances have been made. It is now a fitting tribute to all the people who have helped with this work.

Anthony Burgess 1917-1993
Wrote a Clockwork Orange
Lived in a Tobacconist Shop in Princess Rd. Moss Side

Sir Charles Halle

Charles Halle grave in Weaste Cemetery Manchester

This notice is by the side of the grave

Elizabeth Gaskell
(Framed picture taken in Elizabeth Gaskells House)

Elizabeth Gaskell's House in Plymouth Grove, Moss Side

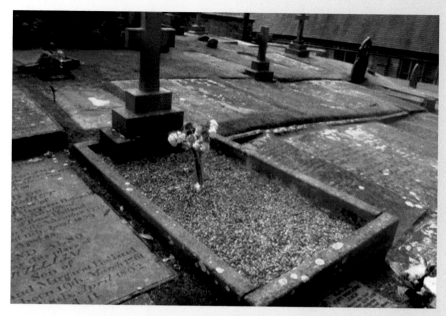

1810-1865
Elizabeth Gaskell grave in Knutsford.
Her husband William was also buried in the same plot. 20 yrs. later

BROOK STREET
CHAPEL

This was built following
the Act of Toleration of 1689,
which allowed Protestant
dissenters to worship in
their own Chapels.
Elizabeth Gaskell, the
Novelist, is buried in
the graveyard.

Elizabeth Guskell's headstone in Knutsford

Emmeline Pankhurst House at 62 Nelson St Moss Side

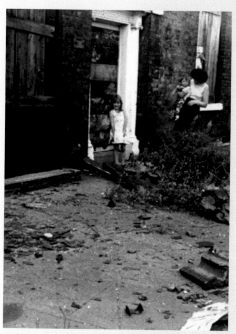

This picture was taken in July 1976 when the house had fallen into a poor state and was badly in need of repair.

Now restored 2018

Emmeline Pankhurst house at 62, Nelson St Moss Side 12/4/18

The house where Mrs. Pankhurst lived is now open to the public as a museum

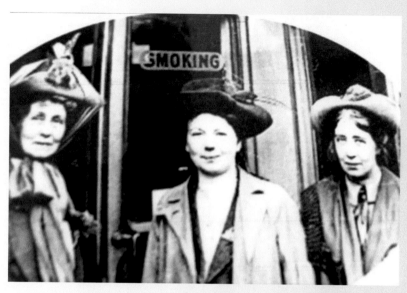

Left to right
Emmeline Pankhurst 1858-1928 with daughters Christabel and Sylvia
Picture taken in the Pankhurst Museum

Emmeline Pankhurst was arrested on several occasions for fighting for the rights of women to be given the vote
(Picture taken in the Pankhurst Museum)

David Lloyd George.

David Lloyd George was born in Moss Side, Manchester in 1863. He was born at an address known as No. 5, New York Place, which was on the corner of Hargreaves Street. Unfortunately this house has now been demolished, as were many other properties in the area.

Although he was born in Manchester, his mother took him Caernarvonshire when his father died. He was brought up by his uncle who worked as a cobbler. Lloyd George went to school in Wales and was a good student learning Latin and French, which would qualify him for legal training.

In 1890 he was elected as Liberal M.P. for Caernarvon and went on to hold a number of top jobs in politics, eventually becoming Prime Minister in 1916. He was the first and only Welshman to hold the office of Prime Minister.

In 1922, Lloyd George was involved in as scandal involving the selling of knighthoods and he resigned as Prime Minister. He did a lot of good work as Prime Minister and he remained in parliament for years after but the Liberal Party never ever ran the government again.

He had made his home in Wales at Ty Newydd, Llanystumdwy, and Caernarvonshire and died at the age of 82 being buried on the banks of the River Dwyfor.

No 5, New York Place, Chorlton on Medlock, Manchester.

This was where Lloyd George was born and lived with his family until he went to his uncle in Caernavon

Sir Fredrick Henry Royce.

Henry Royce was born in Alwalton, near Peterborough in 1863. He was the youngest of five children. His father ran a flour mill but the business failed and they moved to London. In 1872 his father died and Henry went out to work, selling newspapers for W.H. Smiths and delivering telegrams for the Post Office. He returned to London where he worked for the Electic Light and Generator Co. before moving to Liverpool working as the Chief Electrician for a street and theatre lighting company.

In 1884, his big break came when he went into partnership with a friend making domestic electrical fittings in a workshop in Cooke Street, Hulme, Manchester. He lived at a number of addresses in Moss Side at around this time (one of which was 45, Barton St).

He married Minnie Punt, in 1893 and they set up home in Charlton-cum-Hardy before moving to a new house in Knutsford in 1898.

By this time, his business was making dynamos and electrical cranes and by 1903 his fascination for all mechanical items led him to buying a motor car. He wasn't satisfied with the standard of the car and began to improve it.

The first Royce car was made in 1904 but it wasn't until Charles Rolls and Henry Royce had their famous meeting at the Midland Hotel in Manchester to form a partnership that the Rolls Royce came into being.

Rolls, who had a car showroom in London selling imported cars was so impressed with Royce's car that he agreed to take all the cars that could be made so long as they had at least 4 cylinders and would be called Rolls-Royce. This was agreed and a partnership was formed in 1906 being called Rolls-Royce Ltd.

Royce was made an O.B.E. in 1918 and continued working on engine designs until his death in 1933.

This commerative Stone marks the spot where Henry Royce had his workshop in Cooke St and where Royce built his first Rolls-Royce car. The area has now been demolished and this commerative Stone can be seen in Hulme Park

Chapter 23

In the mid 60's the area where we lived was becoming very run down and families were being moved out of their homes and finding new accommodations; sometimes many miles away. The reason behind this was slum-clearance was beginning. It took many years to complete the clearances but bit by bit, streets were being cleared. My friend Malcolm's dad worked as the caretaker at a school near the Poplar Cinema in Hulme and was offered another position as caretaker at a school in Moston. They moved out to Moston, as the job came with a live-in house just across the road from the new school. We used to still meet up for years after his move, until he met a girl from Oldham and got married. My other friend Alan and I still went about together, going to the Snooker Hall on Raby St, Dogs at Belle Vue, Ten-Pin Bowling in Levenshulme and of course football in the parks. Going back to football, my weekends were mainly spent playing football for Yew Tree School on Saturday mornings. Wythenshawe Amatuers on Saturday afternoon and St Clements (By now a proper team in a proper league) on a Sunday. The snooker, dogs, and Ten-Pin Bowling were fitted in around the football. At about this time, I made friends with Ron who went to Yew Tree School.

He was a good footballer and we played in the same teams for Wythenshawe Amatuers and St Clements.

Although Ron lived many miles away in Wythenshawe, he would come to Moss Side and join in with all the events we were involved in. He was very sporty and rekindled my interest in tennis. Again Alexandra Park would be the venue and I would return the compliment by going to his local park (Wythenshawe Park) and playing tennis and pitch and putt (golf). We were both very competitive and games were always very close as we were both reasonable players.

Chapter 24

Leaving Moss Side for Timperley.

Our family moved from Moss Side to Timperley in 1965 as many parts of Moss Side was being demolished. I left Moss Side with a heavy heart. I had loved my life in Moss Side and had started working in an office in Delvino Street, which was very close to our house in Moss Side. The firm I was working for was a plumbers merchants called Whitehead & Sons Ltd.

I had a motorbike to travel from Timperley back to Moss Side daily for work and after work, found myself calling on all my friends who still lived in Moss Side.

As time went on, Whiteheads were given notice that their premises were due for demolition and so they moved to a larger building in Whalley Range. The demolition program was now picking up pace and most of my friends were now disappearing, moving on to pastures new.

Over the years I have gone back to visit Moss Side on many occasions and have tried to piece together where places used to be. Denmark Road Market had gone, Webster Street School had gone, Towlers had gone, St. Clements Church had gone and even the playground where I had scored thousands of goals (situated between Crowborough St, Greenhill St and Webster St) had gone. All that was left was miles of rubble. Even the top end of Greenheys Lane (Princess Rd end) had disappeared and been swallowed up by a massive extension to the Harp Brewery.

Later I discovered that a new Webster Street School had been built on Denmark Road and also a new Princess Road School was built on Alexandra Road. But nothing seems to last forever and Princess Road School has now disappeared altogether.

I was eventually made redundant from Whiteheads in December 1967 as the family firm were closing down. I found a new job in the offices at British Gas in Altrincham and spent the next 30 years working for them.

During my time with British Gas, I used to organize a primary schools soccer tournament for schools in the local area and this became a very successful event for the schools, who adopted it as part of their yearly calendar.

This led me to recall my memories of the past, in and around Moss Side as there were lots of schools in the area. They varied in sizes, but one thing they all had in common, was the formation of memories for each individual pupil.

These memories would stay with them for the rest of their lives.

The school which was right on my doorstep in Moss Side was Webster Street Primary School. Although I never went to this school, most of friends went there and as I mentioned in an earlier chapter, I did go to club nights there.

I recall the caretaker of this school, Mr. Morris, who had a bit of a reputation for playing everything by the book and would not stand for any nonsense. He had quite a large family and lived in the grounds of the school. Some of his children became friends of our group during our teenage years.

I have covered Princess Road School earlier as this was the school which I attended. There was Greenheys Primary School on Great Western Street, Heald Place School, Claremont Road,, St. Marys, St. Margarets, Ducie Avenue, Holy Name to name a few but I'm sure there were lots more.

All these schools (plus more) showed how many children resided in a relatively small plot of land in Manchester and all these children would now have grown up and have their own memories of growing up in and around Moss Side.

I feel sure that their memories would be fairly similar to mine and hopefully this book will bring back some pleasant memories of their own. Occasionally I meet people who lived in Moss Side many years ago and they have very fond tales to tell. They recall names of streets which have long disappeared and tell stories of what it was like for them to live in and around their particular streets.

A visit back to Greenheys/Moss Side in 1973 shows some buildings still standing
Taken from Crowborough St of the playground in 1973
Towlers is on the far left - Webster Street School is on the right

Taken from Greenheys Lane looking down Greenhill St. in 1973. On the left is Webster St School - on the right is
Towlers and just beyond Towlers is the playground

Front entrance to the Old Webster St School

The New Webster St School which is on Denmark Rd. Moss Side

Back entrance of the old Webster St School - taken from Greenhill St - looking down Crowborough St.

A part Map of Moss Side in the 50's - 60's

CONCLUSION

After a long and happy marriage to my wife Pat; shortly before Christmas 2017, Pat passed away, after a 12 month battle with cancer.

To fill in time and adjust to life without Pat, I set about the promise I had made to both my wife and my mother that I would attempt to complete this book.

Although I stated earlier in my book that I am not a great reader; it has given me a great deal of pleasure to use mums newspaper cuttings and notes, photographs and research into making what I hope would have a fairly accurate account of what our life was like when we lived in Moss Side.

There are lots more memories I have of those days and can still remember lots of people who lived in the area before they were moved out.

When the bulldozers moved in and tore down the buildings, we lost so much history and the community spirit was lost forever. I know it is progress and a lot of the buildings were crumbling, but I still feel that too much was destroyed in too short a time.

There are still parts of Moss Side existing which are as I remember it, but these are now few and far between.

OVERALL VIEW OF MOSS SIDE BOOK

Although my mum started writing this book from a historical point of view, she never managed to complete it, as ill health took its toll on her and she passed away in 2009. The book takes in the journey which led our family to Moss Side in Manchester, and when she passed away, I felt the need to finish the book in her memory.

It takes a slight change of direction in so much as my writings are based on my memorize of being brought up in Moss Side in the late 1950's/1960's, rather than mums facts and figures of how Moss Side developed from its early days.

Fortunately I have always liked taking photographs of events and places and some of my pictures have proved to be useful in completing this book.

Moss Side is the perfect example of not being able to go back to view a particular site or building as such a lot of the area was devastated by slum-clearance.

After touring around Moss Side recently, I discovered that most of the smaller streets had disappeared or been altered beyond recognition. New estates had been built on the demolished ground and because of this, the planners could start with a blank canvas and rebuild again. Some major roads still exist and this was helpful in trying to locate where places used to be.

It was quite a surprise to travel along some of these major roads and find certain buildings which had survived the demolition period.

Maybe in another 100 years' time, the whole process will begin again and today's new houses and roads will be changed yet again.

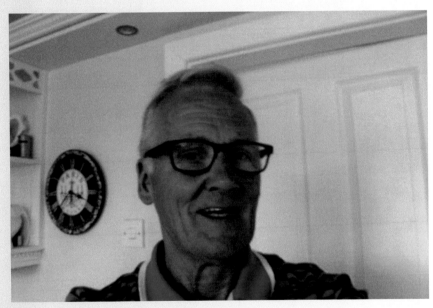

Alan Williams

Printed in the United States
By Bookmasters